W9-DES-007

EXTREME SPORTS

SNOWBOARDING SLOPESTYLE

BY THOMAS K. ADAMSON

EPIC

BELLWETHER MEDIA • MINNEAPOLIS, MN

EPIC

EPIC BOOKS are no ordinary books. They burst with intense action, high-speed heroics, and shadows of the unknown. Are you ready for an Epic adventure?

This edition first published in 2016 by Bellwether Media, Inc.

Library of Congress Cataloging-in-Publication Data

Adamson, Thomas K., 1970-
  Snowboarding Slopestyle / by Thomas K. Adamson.
      pages cm. – (Epic: Extreme Sports)
  Includes bibliographical references and index.
  Summary: "Engaging images accompany information about snowboarding slopestyle. The combination of high-interest subject matter and light text is intended for students in grades 2 through 7"– Provided by publisher.
  Audience: Grades 2 through 7.
  ISBN 978-1-62617-353-8 (hardcover : alk. paper)
  1. Snowboarding–Competitions–Juvenile literature. 2. Obstacle racing–Juvenile literature. I. Title.
  GV857.S57A38 2016
  796.939–dc23
                           2015029850

Printed in the United States of America, North Mankato, MN.

TABLE OF CONTENTS

WARNING

The tricks shown in this book are performed by professionals. Always wear a helmet and other safety gear when you are on a snowboard.

AN OLYMPIC GOLD

Jamie Anderson glides down the slopestyle course. It is her second **run**. She has to score above 92.5 to pass the current leader. Anderson makes smooth landings off her rail slides. Then she gets to the jumps.

MONEY BOOTER

The last jump on a slopestyle course is known as the "money booter."

Her first **trick** is a Cab 720 tail grab. She lands a Switch Backside 540 next. Her run ends with a Frontside 720. The judges give Anderson a score no one beats. She wins gold at the Sochi 2014 Winter Olympic Games!

SLOPESTYLE SNOWBOARDING

Slopestyle lets snowboarders show off their tricks. A slopestyle course starts with a few **obstacles**. Riders slide down rails. They **jib** off walls. Then they spin and flip off huge jumps.

Slopestyle riders have a range of skills and **styles**. They know how to slide down rails smoothly. On jumps they do difficult cab spins and switch tricks.

SNOWBOARDING SLOPESTYLE TERMS

booter—another name for a jump on a slopestyle course

Cab 720 tail grab—a trick in which the snowboarder does two full spins forward in the air with the rear foot in front and one hand holding the end of the board

carve—to turn sharply on a snowboard

Frontside 720—a trick in which the snowboarder spins forward twice in the air

rail slide—a trick in which the snowboarder slides the board down a metal pipe or tube

Switch Backside 540—a trick in which the snowboarder spins backward two and a half times with the back foot forward

SLOPESTYLE HISTORY

Early snowboarders first sped down hills. They carved sharp turns. By the 1990s, many snowboarders were trying tricks. They jumped off tree stumps, stair rails, and other obstacles.

THE SNURFER
An early form of the snowboard was the Snurfer. Sherman Poppen invented the Snurfer in the 1960s.

1997 Winter
X Games

Snowboarding was featured in the first Winter X Games in 1997. The slopestyle events were popular. Fans loved the mix of skills and obstacles.

NEW OLYMPIC EVENT
Snowboard Slopestyle first became an Olympic event in 2014.

15

SLOPESTYLE GEAR

Slopestyle snowboards are **flexible**. This makes them better for hitting obstacles. Slopestyle riders wear helmets to protect them in falls. Goggles shield their eyes.

LOTS OF LAYERS

Snowboarders wear layers of clothing. Layers keep them warm in cold weather. Riders can take layers off if they get too hot.

THE COMPETITION

Slopestyle events have **qualifying rounds**. Riders with the best scores move on to the finals. In the finals, riders usually get two or three runs. Only their best score counts.

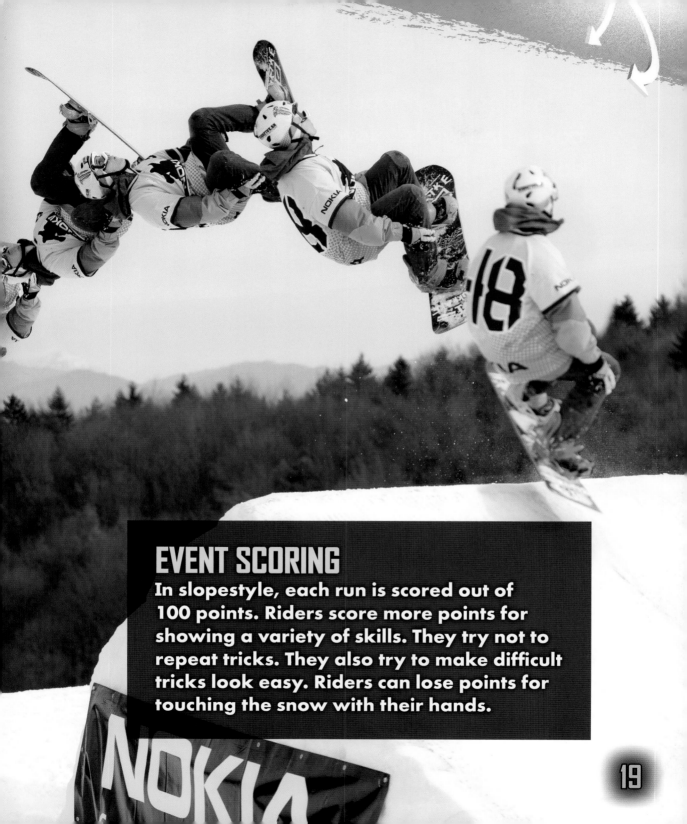

EVENT SCORING

In slopestyle, each run is scored out of 100 points. Riders score more points for showing a variety of skills. They try not to repeat tricks. They also try to make difficult tricks look easy. Riders can lose points for touching the snow with their hands.

Besides rails, slopestyle courses include boxes and walls. New courses are built for each **competition**. This helps riders stay **creative** and keeps fans excited!

LOCAL CULTURE
A huge Russian nesting doll sat in the middle of the slopestyle course at the 2014 Sochi Olympics.

INNOVATOR OF THE SPORT

name: **Shaun White**
birthdate: **September 3, 1986**
hometown: **Carlsbad, California**
innovations: **Won more than 10 X Games gold medals in both superpipe and slopestyle and has two Olympic snowboarding gold medals**

GLOSSARY

competition—an event in which people perform tricks to win

creative—thinking of new ideas

flexible—able to bend

jib—to make contact with an obstacle with the board

obstacles—objects on the slopestyle course that challenge riders

qualifying rounds—early parts of a competition; riders with the highest scores move on to the final rounds.

run—a turn at competing in an event

styles—ways in which something is done

trick—a specific move in a snowboarding slopestyle event

TO LEARN MORE

AT THE LIBRARY

Hile, Lori. *The Science of Snowboarding*. North Mankato, Minn.: Capstone Press, 2014.

Mason, Paul. *Snowboarding*. Chicago, Ill.: Raintree, 2014.

Wiseman, Blaine. *Snowboarding*. New York, N.Y.: Smartbook Media Inc., 2015.

ON THE WEB

Learning more about snowboarding slopestyle is as easy as 1, 2, 3.

1. Go to www.factsurfer.com.

2. Enter "snowboarding slopestyle" into the search box.

3. Click the "Surf" button and you will see a list of related web sites.

With factsurfer.com, finding more information is just a click away.

INDEX